Thawing Tensions
Mindfulness for Deepening Intimacy

Table of Contents

Chapter 1. Introduction

In a world where events often take precedence over emotions, it can be difficult to maintain deeper connections with the ones we love. Welcome to a special report that will change how you approach your relationships: "Thawing Tensions: Mindfulness for Deepening Intimacy." With a refreshing blend of psychological insights and practical advice, this report is your guide to cultivating more profound, trusting relationships using the power of mindfulness. Bursting with relatable examples, expert interviews, and step-by-step mindfulness exercises, it's designed to thaw any icy emotions, fostering open-hearted communication, empathy, and genuine intimacy. Cheer up! The days of disconnectedness are behind you. By investing in this special report, you're embarking on a fulfilling journey towards nurturing more passionate, meaningful connections in your life.

Chapter 2. Understanding Mindfulness: Key Concepts and Misconceptions

Mindfulness is a term that has been buzzing around recently, often hailed as a miracle cure to modern day stress. But what exactly does it mean, and is it really as effective as its proponents claim? Though some misconceptions persist, we are here to uncover its simplicity and profundity.

2.1. Foundations of Mindfulness

At its core, mindfulness is about awareness—an arresting, non-judgmental attention to present-moment experience. Arrayed as a blend of ancient Eastern traditions and psychological principles, mindfulness nudges your consciousness away from habitual, automatic, and often counterproductive behaviors towards a fresh outlook grounded in the 'now.'

The concept, though simple, tends to be overshadowed by a cacophony of assumptions and complex jargon. Clear your mind of what you think you know about mindfulness, and let's get to its roots.

Mindfulness draws its origins from Buddhism, primarily the concept of 'Sati,' which points towards remembering the present moment, free of bias. However, the modern application of mindfulness, often divorced from its spiritual context, leans on the clinical findings of psychology and neuroscience. Research shows that dedicated mindfulness practice can reduce anxiety, stress, and even alleviate symptoms of physical discomfort.

2.2. Misunderstanding Mindfulness

Despite its steam rolling popularity, mindfulness is often misunderstood. Here are a few chart-topping misconceptions:

1. It's about emptying your mind: Contrary to the popular belief, mindfulness isn't about emptying your mind of all thoughts. Rather, the practice encourages observing thoughts without judgment or dissolution into them.

2. You need oodles of time: Sure, retreats or lengthy sessions could be beneficial. But mindfulness is a pervasive mode of being, not an activity. It's about how you do what you do. Scooping out 5 minutes for focused breathing can weave mindfulness into your day.

3. It's a religious practice: While rooted in Buddhism, contemporary mindfulness does not require association with any religious or spiritual belief system.

2.3. Mindfulness in Practice

Mindfulness practice can be as accessible as tuning into the rhythm of your breath, savouring a cup of coffee, or truly listening in a conversation. It's about diverting from autopilot mode and perceiving the fleeting present with curiosity and kindness.

Various techniques can help cultivate mindfulness. Mindfulness-based stress reduction (MBSR), developed by Jon Kabat-Zinn, is an 8-week evidence-based program that offers intensive mindfulness training to assist people with stress, anxiety, depression, and pain.

You can plant the seeds of mindfulness in daily life through formal practices like meditation or yoga, or informal practices, such as mindfully washing dishes, walking, or eating.

2.4. Key Concepts in Mindfulness

1. Awareness: Mindfulness kindles awareness that is simultaneous and direct, uncluttered by fleet-footed judgments. It invites you to embrace a direct experience of the present moment.

2. Non-Judgment: The practice encourages perceiving experiences without labeling them as good or bad. This neutrality cushions against distress linked to negative experiences and brings lucidity to your reactions.

3. Acceptance: Acceptance here doesn't mean resignation but understanding what is, without attempting to change or resist the unfolding event.

4. Mind-Body Integration: Your mind and body are intricately wired. Mindfulness helps integrate and harmonize this mind-body dialogue, fostering holistic health.

5. Impermanence: Mindfulness highlights life's transient nature, underscoring the constant flux of thoughts, feelings, and experiences.

2.5. The Science Behind Mindfulness

Scientific research on mindfulness has surged over the past few decades, showing correlations between mindfulness practice and a variety of emotional, cognitive, and physical benefits.

Neurological studies reveal that mindfulness cultivates brain plasticity, augmenting areas related to attention, emotion regulation, and self-awareness while contracting stress-related regions. Studies also purport benefits such as reduced rumination, stress reduction, boost in working memory, and enhanced focus.

Mindfulness can also spawn emotional and social benefits like fostering empathy and compassion, improving relationship satisfaction, boosting emotional resilience, and buffering against anxiety and depression.

2.6. The Snowball Effect of Mindfulness

Mindfulness isn't an endpoint but a path that opens avenues to other transformative practices. Once you engage with mindfulness, you might find that other practices like compassion, acceptance, gratitude, and forgiveness sprout naturally.

These benefits aren't overnight miracles. Cultivating mindfulness takes patience, consistency, and commitment. Remember, it's a gentle process of coming home to yourself, of recollecting the scattered fragments of your attention to anchor in the 'here' and 'now.'

To unearth the magic of mindfulness, you need to delve beyond the noise of misconceptions and commercialization. Grounded in the reality of the present moment, mindfulness is your faithful ally in navigating the undulating waves of life and nurturing deeper, richer human connections. This is the heart of the matter; this is what we tend to forget so easily amidst the rigors of our routine. With mindfulness, you are not just 'doing' but also 'being'—fully alive and fully present—for what matters the most: your relationships, your passion, your life.

On this note, we hope this chapter steered clarity about mindfulness, paving the way for the following chapters that will together help you thaw those icy temperatures and step into the warmth of trust, openness, and profound intimacy. Remain curious and patient as we explore further.

Chapter 3. Mending Emotional Borders: The link between Mindfulness and Intimacy

Emotional landscape forms the underpinning of any relationship, presenting the deepest contours in the map of love, ranging from peaks of joy to valleys of discontent. This intricate tapestry of emotions often becomes fraught over time, manifesting in the form of stress, disputes, and disconnect – what we term as the "emotional borders."

The key to mending these emotional borders and enhancing intimacy lies in a scientifically-proven approach: mindfulness.

3.1. The Nature of Emotional Borders

Emotional borders signify the invisible yet potent hurdles existing between partners that limit the depth and intensity of shared emotions. These can arise from a plethora of hostilities like misunderstandings, unresolved arguments, and past traumas – effectively encasing your emotional connection in a blanket of frost. Relationships enveloped by thick emotional borders often exhibit shallow communication, limited empathy, and minimal emotional connection.

To break this chain of hostility and to invite warmth into the relationship, it's pivotal to recognize these emotional borders, decode their origins, and navigate solutions. Mindfulness, a consciously centered approach, facilitates this repair job remarkably well.

3.2. Mindfulness: An Explanation

Mindfulness is traditionally rooted in Buddhist meditation practices and has been aptly adopted in modern psychology to tame the wild horses of distressing emotional and mental states. Essentially, it refers to keeping one's attention focused on the present moment, without any judgment or conceptualization.

Imaginatively, consider the mind as a sky churning with thoughts, feelings, and sensations that are similar to passing clouds. Mindfulness encourages regarding these transients objectively, and not the stormy weather that these becloud might suggest.

The practice embraces acceptance of emotions, fostering recognition and understanding rather than repression or denial. This is particularly key when confronting the hard borders of emotional disconnect.

3.3. Mindfulness and Emotional Borders: The Connection

Through mindfulness, you can consciously command your natural stress response. By recognizing and acknowledging feelings or thoughts, you render them powerless over your immediate reactions, fostering level-headedness. Consequently, it aids in handling emotional conflicts, reducing resultant stress, and averting the emotional borders' cementing.

Also, mindfulness fosters empathy – an essential key in fostering relationship intimacy. Mindful people are better attuned to their emotional responses and hence, are more likely to respond considerately to their partner's feelings. Your empathetic responses evoked by mindfulness can ignite the flame of intimacy and connection, thawing the festering emotional borders.

3.4. Mindfulness-Centered Exercises to Mend the Emotional Borders

Next, let's explore constructive mindfulness exercises you can incorporate into your daily routine.

1. **Mindful breathing:** Enabling calming and centering, mindful breathing forms the foundation of mindfulness practice. Even five minutes of focused breathing can yield significant improvements in your emotional clarity, making it an ideal starter practice.

2. **Mindful listening:** The essence of mindful listening is to engage completely with your partner's words - soaking in their voice, message, and underlying emotions, without allowing your thoughts or judgments to interrupt. It encourages patience, understanding, and empathetic responses, ultimately enhancing emotional connection.

3. **Loving-kindness meditation:** This practice radiates well wishes toward yourself and towards others, fostering empathy, forgiveness, and dissolving emotional borders.

Remember, mindfulness is volitional, not a panacea. A single-session cannot dissolve established emotional borders, but persistent practice can undoubtedly build bridges over them.

3.5. Adopting a Mindful Outlook

Adopting a mindful outlook is not confined to meditation cushions or yoga mats. Embed mindfulness in your interactions, conversations, and reactions, thereby fostering deeper, more genuine relationships.

Embrace regular periods of silence to engage with personal feelings or thoughts. The aim is not to control or suppress emotions but to give them space to breathe with unbiased acceptance. Importantly, allow this non-judgmental perspective to seep into your interactions, encouraging open-hearted conversations cast free of blame or values.

Finally, embrace gratitude consciously, noticing the smallest joys brought to you by your partner. Expressing it strengthens emotional ties and fosters an environment conducive to thawing icy tensions.

3.6. Conclusion

Intertwining mindfulness into your daily lives can positively impact your relationships. The path of mindfulness, though simple in understanding, requires deliberate and sustained effort. By incorporating this practice, you're allowing emotions to express themselves freely, fostering empathy, and resolving the emotional borders standing between you and deeper intimacy.

Observe, breathe, and embrace your feelings, appreciating their transient nature and inevitably uncovering what truly makes you more open-hearted and connected. Human bonds, like everything else in the universe, thrive in warmth – the warmth brought forth by mindfulness is a touch away, waiting to be embraced.

Chapter 4. Exploring Barriers to Deep Connection: Breaking Down Emotional Icebergs

Deep and meaningful connections are life's essence, vital to our physical, mental, and emotional well-being. Despite this fact, we often find ourselves disconnected, standing on the other side of an invisible wall, stranded in a sea of misunderstanding and emotional disconnect. The barriers to profound connection are many and varied, much like the massive, unseen parts of the proverbial iceberg lurking beneath the waters of our consciousness.

4.1. Understanding Emotional Icebergs

To understand and overcome those barriers, one must first recognize what an emotional iceberg represents. On the surface, an emotional iceberg is the tip of our conscious understanding of our feelings. It's the part of our emotions that we are aware of, clearly visible and acknowledged. However, beneath the surface lies a vast reservoir of thoughts, feelings, and convictions, unacknowledged and often neglected, the true bulk of our emotional iceberg.

This invisible part consists of deeply ingrained beliefs and childhood experiences, which shape our responses to current situations. Often, these are buried so deep in our psyche; we're not even aware of how profoundly they affect our interactions and relationships. By promoting awareness of these undercurrents, mindfulness can foster understanding and help dismantle these barriers.

4.2. The Role of Emotional Awareness

Emotional awareness is the fundamental step towards breaking down your emotional iceberg. It involves identifying and acknowledging both positive and negative feelings, probing beneath the surface to discover the root causes of these feelings.

With the assistance of mindfulness exercises that focus on body responses, you can heighten your awareness of your emotional responses. For instance, when you have a heated argument with a loved one, acknowledging the rush of adrenaline, rapid heartbeat, or the knots in your stomach, can help you to better understand your emotional state.

Practical exercises include various mindfulness meditation techniques. A simple practice is to spare a few minutes each day in a quiet atmosphere to reflect on your emotions. Close your eyes, take deep calming breaths, and let your thoughts flow freely. Acknowledge whatever emotion surfaces, without judgment or resistance. These exercises aim at developing emotional literacy, a critical part of yielding deeper, more intimate connections.

4.3. Embracing Vulnerability

While the awareness of our emotions is essential, it is equally important to embrace vulnerability. The fear of disclosing our real feelings is another barrier to creating deep connections.

Opening up involves fear of rejection or ridicule; it means showing our most vulnerable side. Yet, it's the raw, shared human experiences that shape the deepest connections.

To conquer this fear, mindfulness helps us become comfortable with the uncomfortable. Again, mindfulness exercises and meditation can foster acceptance of ourselves, our feelings, and situations. It helps us disentangle our self-worth from the fear of judgment or rejection and encourages openness and authenticity.

4.4. Communication: The Key to Connection

Even individuals who are self-aware and open to expressing their feelings can encounter barriers if they fail to communicate effectively. Mindful communication – expressing oneself honestly and listening attentively - presents another opportunity to deepen intimacy.

Active listening, for instance, is about more than simply hearing words. It's about noticing body language, understanding emotions, and recognizing the unspoken messages. During conversations, be present in the moment. Note your reactions and make a conscious effort to empathize with the speaker. Convey your understanding with simple nods or disclosure of personal, similar experiences.

4.5. Walking Towards Emotional Freedom

The journey towards breaking down emotional icebergs comprises consistent efforts, and the barriers may often seem insurmountable. Remember that this journey is a marathon, not a sprint, and self-compassion is necessary. There may be setbacks, but with each barrier overcome, you move one step closer to deeper, more enriching relationships.

As you gain insight into your emotional iceberg and work on dismantling the barriers, remember to celebrate the small victories along the way. Be patient and treat each unveiled emotion or conquered fear as a milestone in your path towards achieving deeper, more meaningful connections in your life.

Through the methods mentioned above, employing emotional awareness, embracing vulnerability, and harnessing the power of communication, we can chip away at our emotional icebergs, effectively breaking down the barriers to deep connection.

Now is the time to turn towards your emotional landscape with an explorer's curiosity. The uncharted terrain might be challenging, but the reward is a life filled with more profound and more gratifying relationships.

Chapter 5. The Emotional Landscape: Recognizing and Navigating Your Feelings

Understanding emotions isn't as intuitive as it may seem. It starts with recognizing the myriad emotions swirling within you and continues with learning how to navigate them. This comprehension is critical not just for personal development, but also for cultivating deeper, more meaningful relationships.

5.1. Emotions: More Than Just Happy, Sad, Angry, or Afraid

Initially, a child learns about basic emotions: happiness, sadness, anger, and fear. However, as we mature, our emotional landscape becomes vastly more complex, intertwined with individual experiences, thoughts, and memories. You don't merely feel sad; you could be feeling melancholy, despondent, or disappointed. Your happiness could be joy, contentment, or relief. Recognizing these nuanced emotions takes practice and mindfulness.

Psychologists believe there are several ways to perceive and express emotions, often represented by layers. The most external layer includes the basic emotions we all understand – happiness, sadness, fear, disgust, anger, and surprise. Beneath this layer, there are secondary and tertiary layers, encompassing subtler shades of emotions, for instance, shame, remorse, exhilaration, and the like. It's important these layers are explored and understood for effective emotional navigation.

5.2. Emotional Recognition: The First Step of the Journey

Being able to correctly identify your emotions is the first step in understanding your emotional landscape. Greater emotional awareness allows for more effective communication and empathic understanding in relationships.

Monitoring your feelings throughout the day is a practical exercise to hone emotional awareness. An emotional diary can help break down your day into specific emotional episodes. For each noteworthy event, write down:

- The situation: What happened? Who was involved?

- The primary emotion: What did you predominately felt?

- The intensity: On a scale of 1-10, how strong was this emotion?

- The response: How did you react?

- Reflection: Consider the situation and your emotional reaction. Was there a better way to respond?

By maintaining an emotional diary, you can increase your emotional vocabulary, recognize emotional patterns, and improve your emotional responses.

5.3. Navigating Your Emotions: Tuning the Emotional Compass

Just as a compass guides us through a physical landscape, our understanding and awareness can help guide us through our emotional one. This requires emotional regulation – a skill that can be improved through intentional practice.

To begin, acknowledge the validity of your emotions. Emotional censorship can lead to denial and further complicates the emotional processing. Instead, accept your feelings, whether they're positive or negative, and remember they come and go like waves.

Practicing mindfulness and meditation can significantly aid in emotional regulation by providing a sense of calm and focus. In this mental state, it's easier to observe your feelings without judgment, enabling watermarked emotions to surface, enhancing your understanding.

Using strategies like deep breathing, progressive muscle relaxation, and visualization during emotional peaks can help counteract physiological responses and restore balance.

5.4. Emotional Responsiveness: React, Don't Suppress

It's essential to differentiate suppression from emotional regulation. Emotional suppression is denying or trying to remove an unwanted sentiment. Unfortunately, it often leads to intensifying the emotion and can have adverse effects on the health and interpersonal relationships. Emotional regulation, on the contrary, is about handling the emotional response in a calm and constructive way.

Creating an action plan for emotional responses can be beneficial. The following is a step-by-step guide for tailoring such a plan:

1. Identify the emotion: Recognize what you're feeling using your cultivated emotional vocabulary.

2. Acknowledge the emotion: Accept your feelings without labeling them as 'bad' or 'good.'

3. Understand the emotion: Explore why you're feeling this emotion. Consider the context and triggers.

4. Evaluate alternatives: Think of multiple ways you could react and

how each would affect your present and future well-being.

5. Choose your action: Select the most beneficial response.

5.5. Implementing Emotional Insights: The Bridge to Improved Relationships

Recognition and regulation of emotions pave the way for deeper relationships by fostering empathy and open-hearted communication. When you understand your emotions, you better comprehend your needs and wants, which supports clarity in expressing your feelings to your partner.

Simultaneously, acknowledging and understanding your partner's emotions cultivates empathy, fostering a more profound emotional connection. Listen carefully to your partner, not just the words they're saying but also the emotions behind them. Understand their emotional journey may be different from yours, and adapt a validating, non-judgmental stance.

This chapter's purpose was to enhance your understanding of the emotional landscape by recognizing and navigating your emotions. The knowledge gained here is stepping stone towards enriching your relationships and ultimately cultivating genuine intimacy.

Chapter 6. Mindful Communication: Conversing with Compassion and Authenticity

Communication is the bedrock upon which relationships are built. Yet, many of us tend to rush through conversations without being fully present. The concept of mindfulness reverses this trend, teaching us how to talk to one another with increased compassion, openness, and authenticity.

6.1. The Importance of Mindful Communication

Mindful communication is not merely about talking; it's about fostering a deep understanding and meaningful connection with the person you're speaking with. When we are mindful, we're fully present in the moment - explicit in our intentions, thoughtful in our words, receptive to the other person's discourse, and unafraid of the silence.

Too often in communication, we're lost in our thoughts, focused on formulating clever rebuttals or mentally predicting what the other person is about to say. In contrast, the practice of mindful communication compels us to listen actively and respond considerately, ensuring that our words and intentions align and that we're truly seeing and valuing the other person.

6.2. Embracing Silence

In mindful communication, silence is not an awkward pause or an absence of speech. Rather, it is an integral component of communication that allows individuals to reflect, comprehend, and be genuinely responsive without feeling rushed. It is through these silences that we find the space and time to deeply understand the other person and their point of view.

Next time you find yourself plunged into a seemingly uncomfortable silence, resist the urge to fill the void with unnecessary chatter. Instead, observe this non-verbal space, as it often carries more meaning than words could ever express. Over time, you'll become comfortable in these silences, discovering a whole new depth of understanding.

6.3. Active Listening

Active listening, another pillar of mindful communication, involves wholeheartedly focusing on the other person's words and non-verbal cues. It's about setting aside your thoughts, judgments, and agendas to make room for understanding the other person's perspective.

Active listening may seem simple, yet it's often overlooked — we're usually too engrossed in formulating our next sentence or rebuttal. However, it's vital to keep in mind that authentic conversations are not a battleground of words. They require genuine efforts of understanding, empathizing, and reacting thoughtfully.

6.4. The Power of Non-Judging

We all bring our past experiences, prejudices, and biases into our conversations, which can color our judgment of others and obstruct genuine communication. To overcome this, it's essential to foster a mindset of non-judging.

When you make a conscious effort to let go of your preconceived notions and judgments, you open up a space for authentic and compassionate communication and learn to see the other person without the veil of your biases. This not only deepens your understanding of them but also builds trust and facilitates smoother conversation.

6.5. The Role of Empathy

Empathy is about putting yourself in the other person's shoes, allowing you to understand their feelings and perspectives deeply. An empathetic conversation involves suspending your view temporarily and entering the speaker's frame of reference without trying to challenge or dilute it.

Remember that empathy does not obligate you to agree with the views of others. Instead, it means acknowledging and validating their feelings and perspectives as real and significant, irrespective of your personal take on the matter. This mutual respect for perspectives makes empathetic conversations genuine and authentic.

6.6. Respond, Don't React

In an engaging discussion, you may sometimes feel the urge to briskly react or argue against a viewpoint that does not align with yours. When faced with such a situation, mindfulness urges us to 'respond', not 'react.'

Remember that reactions are instant, driven by biases and emotions. In comparison, responses are thoughtful, deliberate, and conscientious. When you respond, you take the time to understand the perspective fully, absorb it, and then mirror it back in a careful, respectful manner.

Mindful communication, therefore, becomes an act of balance —

balancing your need to express with your readiness to understand, your desire to be heard with your willingness to listen. As you start to internalize these tenets of mindful communication, you'll notice a gradual shift in the way you communicate, enhancing the depth and quality of your conversations and relationships.

In the pursuit of mindful communication, remember there is no right or wrong way to practice it. It's a journey of learning, unlearning, and cultivated patience.

Each conversation is a unique dance, intricately choreographed with individual emotions, experiences, biases, and limitations. And it's the blend of mindful listening, empathetic understanding, and authentic conversation that makes this dance harmonious and a beautiful journey of connection.

Mindfulness thus serves as an invaluable tool, empowering you to engage in deeper, more compassionate interactions, leading to a life filled with richer relationships and profound intimacy.

Chapter 7. Harnessing Empathy: The Heart of Meaningful Relationships

Empathy represents a potent bonding agent, a lubricant that nurtures relationships and enables genuine connection. Irrespective of age, culture, or lifestyle, it is the universal language that invites us into another's world, prompting us to hold space for their emotions without judgment. Cultivating empathy offers insight into others' perspectives, reinforcing trust and diminishing relational friction.

7.1. The Essence of Empathy

Fundamentally, empathy is the ability to understand someone else's feelings as if we were having them ourselves. It allows us to share another person's experiences subtly and has a remarkable ability to unite us as humans. Empathy not only heightens our emotional intelligence but also fosters compassion, kindness, and understanding, all of which strengthen relationships.

7.2. Distinction Between Empathy and Sympathy

Empathy and sympathy are frequently misinterpreted as the same emotion. Sympathy, however, is feeling compassion or sorrow for someone's misfortune, whereas empathy involves placing oneself in another's shoes and experiencing their emotions alongside them. It's essential to differentiate these feelings as empathy builds stronger bonds compared to sympathy, which merely acknowledges another's hardship.

7.3. Recognizing Empathy: An Exploration

Empathy can be categorized into cognitive empathy and emotional empathy: Cognitive empathy, or perspective-taking, encompasses understanding another's thoughts or perspectives, while emotional empathy involves sharing and resonating with their emotions.

To nurture these forms of empathy, consider:

6+ | Cognitive Empathy

a | **Acknowledge Differences**: Everyone perceives the world differently, influenced by their backgrounds, experiences, and beliefs. Recognize these distinctions without judgment to empathize sincerely. a | **Practice Active Listening**: Engage in focused listening without interruptions or interjecting your perspectives. a | **Ask Questions**: Inquire about their experiences or emotions to promote a deeper understanding.

6+ | Emotional Empathy

a | **Evaluate Non-verbal Messages**: Understand emotions communicated through body language, tone, or facial expressions. a | **Reflect Emotion**: Mirror their emotions back to them to validate their feelings. a | **Share in Emotion**: Allow yourself to personally resonate with their emotions.

7.4. Empathy in Practice

Empathy finds true expression when we incorporate it into our daily interactions. A fruitless exercise if confined to understanding, empathy demands actionable manifestations to have any positive impact on relationships.

Empathy in practice could involve:

Acknowledging Others' Feelings: By verbally acknowledging another's feelings, you can validate their emotional experience, which can lead to deeper conversations more intimate connections.

Expressing Understanding: Utilize phrases like 'I can understand you feel...' to convey your empathy.

Showing Patience and Understanding: Empathy also demands patience, especially when dealing with highly emotional situations.

Developing empathy as a relational skill requires consistent practice and deep personal introspection. Recognizing the inherent emotional diversity among us prompts a richer, empathic understanding of those around us.

7.5. Empathy as a Foundation of Intimacy

The link between empathy and intimacy is particularly significant, as empathy helps nourish deep, emotional connections, fostering feelings of safety, comfort, and closeness in relationships. It promotes heartfelt conversations, de-escalates conflicts, and is instrumental in providing emotional support.

7.6. Interviews with Experts

Interviews with renowned psychologists, therapists, and researchers emphasized the role of empathy across different relationship types, affirming its importance in building, nurturing, and sustaining meaningful emotional bonds.

7.7. Enhancing Empathy: Exercises and Techniques

For honing your empathic prowess, consider mindfulness exercises designed to push beyond your emotional barriers and venture into others' emotional worlds.

1. Mindful Listening: Engage in active listening, paying full attention to the speaker without forming responses in your mind. This practice improves cognitive empathy.

2. Emotional Literacy: Strive to label and understand the broad spectrum of emotions. Drawing or journaling can be helpful tools in this process.

3. Perspective-Taking Exercises: Try to view situations from different perspectives to hone cognitive empathy. Role-playing or reading literature are creative methods to practice.

4. Empathy Map: Mapping out what others might be thinking, feeling, and experiencing can help develop emotional empathy.

5. Mindful Breathing: Use mindful breathing to remain calm during emotionally charged situations or conversations. This helps maintain a level head, which is essential for empathetic responses.

Understanding and practicing empathy is a significant step towards achieving deeper, more meaningful connections in relationships. An ally in navigating the complex emotional landscape of human connection, empathy provides the necessary support and understanding required to build lasting bonds. Remember, the journey of empathy is ongoing, lifelong and utterly rewarding. Life gains more depth, richness, and meaning when we make the choice to understand, respect, and care for the emotions of others as our own.

Chapter 8. Meditation Techniques for Enhancing Intimacy

Meditation is a form of mindfulness that can be practiced in various ways, each with its unique benefits. For the purpose of enriching relationships, there are several mindfulness meditation techniques that can be particularly helpful. Incorporating these into your life can not only contribute to individual growth but also significantly enhance intimacy and trust between you and your loved ones.

8.1. The Basics: Understanding Meditation

Meditation involves quieting the mind to focus on the present moment, reducing stress and anxiety while bringing about a deeper understanding of one's thoughts and feelings.

In the context of relationships, it allows us to pause and reflect on our behavior and emotions, fostering understanding and empathy toward our partners. It cultivates positive communication, facilitates conflict resolution, and promotes shared experiences that deepen intimacy.

Many people are daunted by the thought of meditation, believing it to be too complex or time-consuming. However, it is quite manageable once you understand the core techniques and principles. Start meditating in small increments and gradually build up as you become more comfortable and familiar with the practice.

8.2. Mindful Breathing for Connection

Perhaps one of the most straightforward and widely practiced forms of meditation is mindful breathing. This technique involves focusing your attention solely on your breath, bringing you into the present moment and promoting calmness and clarity. Practicing this form of meditation together with your partner can significantly increase feelings of connection.

To practice mindful breathing: . Sit comfortably, with your backs upright but not stiff. . Close your eyes and take a few deep breaths, noticing how the breath flows in and out of your body. . As you exhale, imagine any stress or tension leaving your body. As you inhale, visualize peaceful energy entering your body. . If your attention wanders, no need to worry. Acknowledge the distraction without judgment and return your focus to your breath.

8.3. Sharing Silence to Deepen Intimacy

Sharing silence can also be a profoundly intimate experience. Just being in the same space with a loved one, absorbed in your breathing and thoughts, can create a sense of unity and mutual understanding.

This might seem a bit unconventional, but practicing stillness and silence together can lead to a deeper bond. It encourages you both to be more present, more aware of each other's existence, and more open to the energy between you two.

To share silence with a partner, set aside a specified time daily where you both sit together in quietude. Focus on your breath and let the silence naturally unfold the non-verbal facets of your relationship.

8.4. Metta Meditation for Building Empathy

Metta, or loving-kindness meditation, is another excellent practice for enhancing relationships. It involves consciously sending goodwill, kindness, and warmth towards others by silently repeating a series of mantras.

The standard mantras are: . May I be safe. . May I be healthy. . May I be happy. . May I live with ease.

After you have directed these statements towards yourself, you then extend them towards your partner, other loved ones, acquaintances, and ultimately even to those with whom you have had conflicts. This practice can foster empathy and bridge gaps by promoting understanding and care.

8.5. Partnered Visualization Technique

Visualization meditation involves focusing your mind on specific images or scenarios. Practicing this with a partner can be a powerful way to deepen your connection.

You could visualize peaceful scenarios or recall shared happy moments. This technique not only brings positivity and serenity into your relationship but also serves as a reminder of the love that binds you. Sharing these visualizations can allow you to mutually immerse in a sense of happiness and connection.

8.6. Mindful Touching

Physical contact is another facet of connection that mindfulness meditation can enhance. Simple actions like holding hands or giving a loving touch can foster a sense of comfort, security, and connection.

In mindful touching, you and your partner hold hands or embrace and sharpen your attention to the sensations of the touch. Recognize the warmth, the pressure, and the comfort that the contact provides. This practice can build a profound connection and a deep sense of shared presence.

Remember, meditation is not a one-size-fits-all solution. It is an ongoing practice, and it may take time to see progress. For best results, adapt these techniques to fit your circumstances and comfort levels, and be sure to approach it with consistency, patience, and an open heart.

Chapter 9. Practical Exercises: Mindfulness Activities For Two

Diving into the practical realm of relationship-building and emotional connectedness, we present a series of exercises crafted with mindfulness at their core. These activities are designed to be shared with a partner, a loved one, or anyone you wish to deepen your bonds with. From simpler, small daily habits to more profound and transformative practices, these exercises offer a diverse range of options to suit each unique relationship.

9.1. Mindful Dialogue

Initiating a mindful dialogue involves active listening and presence of mind, an openness to perceive and communicate with your partner without judgment. It's a chance to explore your thoughts and feelings, and likewise, to understand your partner's mental and emotional landscape.

The practice is simple. Decide on a quiet and calm place for the dialogue to occur. Set aside a designated period for the conversation, with each participant getting an equal share. As one speaks, the other listens without interruption or judgment, focusing simply on understanding the speaker's perspective. After the speaking turn, the listener may respond mindfully, either addressing the points made or sharing their own feelings. Encourage clarification instead of assumption, ensuring that both parties understand each other.

9.2. Mindful Eating

Mindful eating encourages you to focus on the experience of eating, appreciating every flavor, texture, and sensation. This exercise can transform a routine meal into a shared event that promotes bonding and mindfulness.

To practice mindful eating, prepare a meal together, taking turns to taste each dish during the cooking process. Discuss your experiences, the flavors, the smells, and how they make you feel. During the meal, eat slowly, savoring each bite, discussing your experiences with each other. Creating this shared culinary journey can enhance your emotional and sensory connections.

9.3. Mindful Breathing

Breath is a vital force, an expression of life's ebb and flow. Mindful breathing offers a chance to connect with your partner on a deeply tranquil level.

Sit comfortably with your backs against each other and begin to breathe deeply, feeling each other's breaths. Try synchronizing your breathing pattern; this encourages hormonal and energetic compatibility. Quietly reflect on the person behind you, the shared breath, and the shared life force.

9.4. Joint Meditation

A joint meditation session not only deepens your mindfulness practice but also helps forge a stronger emotional bond with your partner.

Choose a quiet, serene spot where you can sit comfortably, preferably in low lighting. Join hands and begin your chosen meditation method. Have a mental intention of connecting with your partner at an emotional and spiritual level. Don't rush this process. Afterward, discuss your experiences and feelings.

9.5. Mindful Walking

Taking a walk together with a mindful approach can be an enriching and grounding experience.

Choose a familiar or new path. Walk slowly, taking in the sensations of every step, how your body moves, the sounds and aromas around you. Do this silently initially, and then share your experiences with your partner. Seeing the world through your partner's perspective can open up new dimensions in your relationship.

9.6. Building Shared Goals

Working toward shared goals helps build trust and unity. Creating shared goals requires clear communication, compromises at times, and celebrating each other's accomplishments.

Sit together, write down your personal goals and share them with each other. Identify any common areas and discuss how you can support each other in these. Create a plan of action and be each other's cheerleader. Revisit these goals periodically, reflecting on your progress and celebrating achievements.

The purpose of these mindfulness activities is to boost empathy, acceptance, and understanding within your relationship. They allow you to nurture your bonds, create beautiful shared experiences, and build a strong foundation. They encourage mutual growth, enhancing not only your relationship but your personal development too. Remember, the goal of mindfulness is not to achieve perfection but to keep growing, learning, and evolving together. And through that evolution, a deeply intimate connection is undoubtedly achievable.

Chapter 10. Guided Mindfulness: Daily Routines for a Vibrant Relationship

Mindfulness - the practice of being present and aware without judgment - has been lauded by countless psychologists, mental health experts, and relationship gurus as a game-changing tool for bringing vibrancy and connection to any relationship. It all begins with identifying and incorporating it into your everyday routines.

10.1. Mastering the Art of Mindful Mornings

Starting your day with mindfulness will set a positive tone for the entirety of your day. Allow us to guide you through a simple, yet incredibly effective, daily routine for mindfulness.

1. **Mindful Wakening:** Start the day by taking a few deep, calming breaths. As you awaken, focus on the sensation of your breath, the softness of your sheets, and the sound of your surroundings. Let these sensations ground you in the present moment.

2. **Gratitude Journaling:** Sit in a quiet, comfortable spot and jot down three things you are grateful for. They don't need to be grand - it can be as simple as feeling thankful for a peaceful night's sleep or the warmth of the sun.

3. **Mindful Activity:** Devote time to a mindful activity such as yoga, tai chi, or even a quiet walk. These activities not only increase your awareness but also give a positive boost to your day.

10.2. Being Present in Routine Activities

Routine activities offer a rich opportunity for mindfulness because they ground us in the present. Here are clever ways to turn your routine activities into mindfulness exercises:

1. **Mindful Eating:** Savor your meals. Appreciate the textures and flavors, and think about where they came from. This approach slows you down, aids digestion, and opens a new world of flavors.

2. **Mindful Cleaning:** Cleaning can be a mindful endeavor. Pay attention to every sweep or scrub, focus on the details, and let your mind relax with the monotonous, clear goal of cleaning.

3. **Mindful Commuting:** Too many people lose countless minutes to mindless commuting. Instead, enjoy the journey. Notice the view, savor the little moments that make your journey unique, and breathe.

10.3. Applying Mindfulness to Interactions

Our interactions can be fraught with misunderstandings. Applying mindfulness to your interactions helps you relate effectively with other people. Let's discuss how:

1. **Active Listening:** Often, we don't listen to respond; we listen to react. Active listening is about fully being present in the conversation, not preparing your rebuttal. It feels empathetic and open, creating space for real connections.

2. **Mindful Speaking:** By being mindful of our words, we convey our thoughts more clearly and help prevent misunderstandings. Think before you speak, consider your words carefully, and

communicate compassionately.

3. **Checking-in Often:** Check-in with your partner often by asking open-ended questions about their day, feelings, or thoughts. This will foster open communication and make your partner feel loved and understood.

10.4. Mindful Evenings and Nights

Ending your day with mindfulness can help you rest better. A nightly mindfulness routine might include:

1. **Reflective Journaling:** Reflect upon the day, pen down your learnings or any emotions you experienced.

2. **Mindful Activities:** Engage in calming activities like reading a book or taking a warm bath while avoiding screens.

3. **Mindful Silence:** End the day with a few minutes of silence, focusing on your breath to calm your mind and body for a restful sleep.

Each routine, activity and interaction presents a chance to turn an ordinary moment into a mindful one. With consistency and conscious effort, these simple practices can create a profound, positive impact on your relationships, helping you and your loved ones draw closer. Remember to be patient with yourself, change takes time. Start small, maybe with a mindful morning routine, and gradually incorporate mindfulness into all hours of your day and all aspects of your life.

Chapter 11. Beyond Resets: A Lifetime of Authentic Connection

Many of us are familiar with the term "reset." In technology, it means bringing a system back to zero. In relationships, however, resets are not as straightforward. Yes, a reset can mean wiping the slate clean, letting go of past hurts, misunderstandings, and starting afresh. Yet, relationships are not machines; they are collections of shared experiences, emotions and memories - both good and bad. Instead, we should strive for authentic, long-lasting connections with our loved ones.

11.1. The Fallacy of Relationship Resets

Pause for a moment and visualize your relationship as a garden. If it's overrun by weeds, you wouldn't tear out everything - all the beautiful flowers and plants - just to get rid of the weeds. Rather, you would carefully extricate them, ensuring the beauty you've grown stays intact. Similarly, in relationships, it isn't wise to erase everything and start afresh just because of a few disagreements or misunderstandings.

Simply pressing a 'reset' button does not help you to understand the root cause of your conflicts or tensions. Without an understanding of why problems arise, there's a high probability that they will reoccur in future. Thus, it's important to recognize, understand, and navigate the ups and downs, instead of simply trying to avoid them.

11.2. Unfolding Authentic Connection

To create a lifetime of authentic connection with someone, you must be prepared to embolden vulnerability, bolster patience, and foster understanding. These aren't switches to be flipped on; these are seeds to be nurtured.

1. Embrace Vulnerability: Being vulnerable means opening yourself up to the possibility of hurt. It involves sharing your true feelings, fears, hopes, and desires without any guarantee of being fully understood or accepted. It might seem scary but being vulnerable is the first step towards building deeper connections.

2. Practice Patience: More than waiting, patience is about how you wait and what you do while waiting. It's about maintaining a positive attitude during the process, even when things are tough. Relationships require this kind of patience where you need to give each other enough space and time to grow.

3. Foster Understanding: As human beings, we all yearn to be understood by someone who can see us just as we are, without judgment or harsh criticism. Hence, strive to exercise empathy and develop an understanding attitude towards your partner.

11.3. Mindfulness as the Key

Creating authentic connections share a common thread with mindfulness - both necessitate a focus on the present. Mindfulness zeroes in on experiencing this very moment, without judgment or distraction. It's about accepting and appreciating things the way they are.

Here's an illustration: Imagine you're walking with a loved one. They might piece together words differently or might stop to appreciate a blooming flower while you're more focused on the path ahead.

Practicing mindfulness will help you remain patient in that pause, allow you to see the flower from their perspective - appreciating that difference, instead of being annoyed by it.

The conversation can continue without needing to brush off or pressure each other to move along too quickly. There's no rush. Through mindfulness, you can create room for understanding, patience, and authenticity in your connections.

11.4. Exercises for a Lifetime Connection

So, let's roll up our sleeves and dive into simple exercises that you can start with today for building deeper bonds in your relationships.

1. Mindful Listening: This practice is about being completely present when someone else is talking. Start with a simple conversation, focusing on their words completely. You might observe that the conversations become more meaningful and heartfelt.

2. Loving Kindness Meditation: This is a meditation practice that involves focusing on developing feelings of goodwill, kindness, and warmth towards others. Spend a few minutes daily visualizing positive energy for your loved one. You'll be surprised by how this simple exercise transforms your relationship.

3. Mindful Acknowledgment: This involves expressing appreciation towards your loved ones. It's about acknowledging the little things they do, their efforts, the value they bring to your life. This not only makes them feel valued but builds respect and understanding.

Building a lifetime of authentic connections cannot happen in a day, but by focusing on the present, embracing vulnerability, practicing patience, and fostering understanding, we can begin an enriching journey that elevates our relationships to a much deeper level. And remember, practising mindfulness is a continuous process. Be dedicated, patient, and genuine - the connections you'll forge will be lifelong and invaluable.